|||||||||| |||| |||||||||||||||||

D0326170

Gift Tage

To:_____

From:_____

Please place your photo here.

Grandpa, Tell Me Your Memories...

Created by Kathleen Lashier

Copyright © 1992, 2006, Linkages

Linkages

To contact the author:

Linkages Memory Journals • P.O. Box 8282 • Des Moines, IA 50301
888-815-9063
www.mymemoryjournals.com

Printed in the U.S.A.
by G&R Publishing Co.

ISBN-13: 978-1-56383-038-9
ISBN-10: 1-56383-038-8

Distributed by:

507 Industrial Street • Waverly, IA 50677
800-887-4445 • Fax 800-886-7496

What was your day and date of birth?

January 1

Where were you born?
Be specific.

January 2

Do you know any other circumstances of your birth (who was present, who delivered, etc.)?

If you have a childhood picture for me, put it in this space.

January 4

Name your brothers and sisters and their years of birth.

January 5

What was your mother's full name?

January 6

What were your mother's date, place and circumstances of birth?

January 7

What was your father's full name?

January 8

*What were your father's
date, place and circumstances of birth?*

January 9

*What did your father
do for a living?*

January 10

Did your mother work outside the home?

January 11

Name all the street addresses you can recall and/or all the communities you've lived in and years there.

January 13

Tell a nickname your family gave you and how you got it.

January 14

Tell of any other nicknames in your family.

Tell a fond memory
of your Grandpa.

January 16

*Tell a fond memory
of your Grandma.*

January 17

Tell about a favorite Aunt.

January 18

Tell about a favorite Uncle.

January 19

Relate an experience or memory of a cousin.

January 20

Did any relatives ever live with you? If not, then relate another memory of cousins, aunts or uncles.

In what way did your mother usually discipline?

*How did your
father discipline?*

January 23

Tell about the naughtiest thing you ever did.

January 24

If you got caught,
describe the consequences.

January 25

Did you ever see a President or Vice-President in person? Which of the Presidents in your lifetime has been your favorite and why?

Did you ever have an imaginary friend?

January 27

What did you and your brothers and/or sisters fight about the most?

Tell about an experience or event that drew you together.

January 29

Tell about the worst winter storm that you can remember as a child.

What did you use to go sledding down a hill in the snow?

January 31

What extras did you use for your snowman's face, buttons, arms, hat, etc?

February 1

*Tell of someone you envied,
and why.*

February 2

Do you remember the first movie you ever saw and who starred in it?

February 3

*What have been some of
your very favorite movies?*

February 4

How did you first
smash a finger?

February 5

Who was the most famous person you ever met as a child?

Tell about someone who had a big influence on your life.

February 7

Tell about another influential person in your life.

February 8

Tell about a big lie you told.

February 9

*Tell about your first
favorite television shows.*

February 10

Who was your first girlfriend?

February 11

Tell about the Valentine's Day festivities at your school.

February 12

Tell about a special valentine you once gave.

February 13

Tell about a special valentine you once received.

February 14

Tell about your first date.

February 15

Tell about your first kiss.

February 16

What was your favorite meal as a child?

February 17

Tell about family reunions in your childhood.

February 18

What do you remember as
your favorite subject in school?

*What do you remember as
your least favorite school subject?*

February 20

What is the biggest problem you remember having in Grade School?

February 21

What is the biggest problem
you remember having
in Jr. High School?

February 22

What is the biggest problem
you remember having
in Sr. High School?

February 23

Tell about a great victory or personal success from your school days.

February 24

Did you and your friends ever have a secret hide-out?

February 25

Tell about a favorite restaurant or public place where you and your friends liked to gather.

Tell about the best pet you ever had.

Tell about other pets you had.

February 28

*Tell about being in a
school play or program.*

March 1

Tell about a school principal you remember.

March 2

Did you ever pretend to be sick as an excuse to stay home from school?

March 3

Did you ever get in trouble for saying a bad word?

March 4

Tell about how you spent your Saturdays during the school years.

March 5

Tell about how you spent your Sundays.

March 6

*What was the naughtiest
or meanest thing you
remember doing in school?*

March 7

What were the consequences?

March 8

Tell of a difficult essay or term paper assignment.

March 9

What radio programs or stations were your favorites?

March 10

Tell of a childhood illness.

March 11

Did your parents have a favorite remedy for when you were sick or hurt?

March 12

Did kids ever tease you and why?

March 13

*Do you remember
your first pizza?*

March 14

If you went to college, tell which college you chose and why.

March 15

*Tell your major and
how you chose it.*

March 16

Did people wear green on St. Patrick's Day?

March 17

*Do you have any other
memories of St. Patrick's Day
as a youth?*

March 18

If you ever hitch-hiked, explain.

March 19

What do you remember as your favorite time of year? Why?

March 20

Describe some household chores you had as a child.

March 21

Describe some outside chores.

March 22

Which chore did you dislike the most and how did you try to get out of it? Did you have a favorite chore?

March 23

What bones have you
broken and how?

March 24

Did you ever need stitches?

March 25

*Do you have any other good
stories about being injured?*

March 26

*Tell about an experience
at the doctor's office.*

March 27

Tell about an experience at the dentist's office.

March 28

Name your best school friends.

March 29

Tell of a nickname given
to you by friends or classmates.
How did you get it?
How did you feel about it?

March 30

What were some crazy names or nicknames in your school?

Do you have a good
April Fool's Day story?

April 1

Tell about a practical joke or prank you played on someone.

April 2

*Tell about a practical joke
or prank someone played on you.*

April 3

Did you make your own kites?
Tell about kite-flying in your youth.

April 4

As a child, what did you want to be when you grew up?

April 5

What was your best talent?
What other things were
you really good at doing?

April 6

Did you ever bring home or try to adopt a wild animal?

*Make up a limerick
about yourself.*

There once was a...

April 8

Make up a limerick about me.

There once was a...

April 9

*Relate a favorite
spring memory.*

April 10

*Did your Mom or Dad
ever find something you had hidden?*

April 11

Share a memory of going to church as you were growing up.

April 12

Share a memory about a church social activity.

April 13

(If the following Easter topics do not apply, please share your special Holiday memories and traditions.)

Tell about an Easter Egg hunt.

*If your family went to
Easter Sunrise services, tell about it.*

April 15

Tell about any other Easter tradition.

When you played make-believe, what did you pretend?

If you could return to your childhood, what would you do differently?

April 18

Is there anything you would do differently as a teenager?

Did you ever write something that you were really proud of?

April 20

What is the best book you ever read as a youth?

Since you've grown, what has been your favorite book?

April 22

Have you ever had a superstition?

Tell about the first time you were ever behind the wheel of a car.

April 24

Where were your best hide-and-seek places?

April 25

*Did you ever take anything
that wasn't yours?*

April 26

What did you do with it?
Did you get caught?

April 27

Do you have a story about a big surprise?

April 28

What childhood fear
do you remember?

April 29

Tell about a
May Day tradition.

April 30

What were May Baskets
made of and what did they contain?

May 1

How much do you remember paying for an ice cream cone?

May 2

Did you have a treehouse?

May 3

Were you ever bitten by a dog?

May 4

Did your Mother ever make a special gift for you?

May 5

Tell a favorite memory of your mother.

May 6

*Tell about some good advice
your mother gave you.*

May 7

Relate your family Mother's Day traditions...or tell me more about the kind of person your mother was.

May 8

What did you learn
from your mother?

May 9

Name some popular hit songs from your youth.

May 10

What was your favorite
singing group or band?

May 11

Tell a favorite singer and a song that he/she sang?

What kind of dances did you do as a youth?

*Tell about the first dance
you ever went to.*

*Did your high school have a
prom or formal dance?*

May 14

Describe your military experience or that of someone in your family.

May 15

Share some memories involving a war during your childhood or youth.

May 16

May 17

If you have another photograph of you as a youth, place it here.

May 18

*What early childhood rhymes
or songs do you remember?*

May 19

What year did you graduate from high school? What do you recall about your feelings, emotions, hopes and dreams at this time of your life?

May 20

May 21

Tell about your graduation exercises or traditions. How many students were in your graduating class?

Did you have homework during your school years?

May 23

What was the dumbest stunt pulled by you and a brother or sister?

May 24

Were there consequences?

May 25

Tell about Memorial Day traditions during your youth.

Share a special memory
of Memorial Day.

May 27

Did you play a musical instrument?

May 28

*Tell about the closest friend
you had in childhood.*

May 29

Is there anything you have now that you have kept from your childhood?

May 30

*Do you have any
good bathtime stories?*

May 31

*Did you have a favorite
nature place you liked to explore?*

June 1

*Describe a place you
liked to go to be alone.*

Did you ever
sleep under the stars?

June 3

Tell about hot dog or marshmallow roasting.

June 4

*Did you ever
go on a camp out?
Tell about it.*

June 5

*Did you ever
go on a snipe hunt?*

June 6

*Did you have a favorite
snack that you made at home?*

June 7

Tell about one of the
first meals you ever prepared?

Tell about a strange person that lived in your town.

What was your first job?
How much were you paid?

Tell about any other paying jobs you held as a youth.

*Were you ever chased
by some animal?*

June 12

If you were ever in a parade, tell about it.

June 13

Tell another memory about a parade.

June 14

*Share a childhood memory
about a death that affected you.*

June 15

Relate your happiest memory as a youth.

June 16

How did you learn to swim?

June 17

Where did you go swimming?

June 18

Tell a favorite memory of your father.

June 19

Tell about some good advice your father gave you.

June 20

*Did your father ever make
a special gift for you?*

June 21

Relate your family Father's Day traditions...or tell me more about the kind of person your father was.

June 22

What did you learn from your father?

June 23

*Did you ever
go skinny-dipping?*

Did you ever make mud pies?

June 24

Did you ever go barefoot in the summer? If so, relate a painful experience about stepping on something.

June 25

As a youth, did you do any craft, sewing, stitching or needlework?

June 26

Tell about a bike you had.

Tell about your
first very own car.

June 28

Did you ever have or make a swing?

June 29

Tell about seeing something you thought was very beautiful.

June 30

Describe an outside game you made up.

July 1

*Describe an inside
game you made up.*

July 2

What kind of fireworks did people have when you were a youth?

July 3

Tell about Independence Day traditions of your childhood.

July 4

*Do you have a special
July 4th that you remember most?*

July 5

Did you ever go to carnivals or amusement parks? Where?

July 6

What kinds of rides and games
were there? How much did they cost?

July 7

Tell about any State Fair
or County Fair experiences.

Tell about going to a circus,
a Chautauqua, or
a hometown celebration/festival.

July 9

*Tell any favorite
summertime memory.*

July 10

Did you go fishing, hunting or trapping in your youth?

*Tell about your biggest
or best catch.*

July 12

Do you remember having a favorite candy? How much did it cost?

Share a horse-riding story.

July 14

Share a memory about going on a picnic.

July 15

What kinds of party games or party activities were popular?

July 16

Share a memory involving a heatwave or drought.

July 17

What did you do to stay cool?

July 18

*What was your favorite
holiday of the year?*

July 19

*Share a birthday
party memory.*

July 20

Tell about the neatest shoes you ever owned as a youth.

*Share a memory
about a power outage.*

July 22

Relate a memory involving a flood or cloudburst.

Relate a memory of a tornado, hurricane or destructive wind.

July 24

_What memories do you have
of lightning or thunder
during your childhood?_

Share a special memory about riding in a boat.

July 26

*Tell about a
family vacation trip.*

July 27

Share the best vacation experience you can recall.

July 28

Share the most unpleasant vacation experience you can recall.

July 29

Do you have any other memories about a river, lake or beach to share?

Tell a memory about riding on a ferry, bus, train or plane.

July 31

Describe a proud moment from your childhood.

August 1

Describe your childhood home.

August 2

Describe your neighborhood.

August 3

Tell about your bedroom.

August 4

Tell a memory about having company at your house, or of a family party.

August 5

Tell about board games you played as a child.

August 6

*Tell about card games
you played.*

*Do you have any knowledge
of how your first name was chosen?*

August 8

Do you have any knowledge about the origins of your family name?

August 9

*Tell about a time
when you got lost.*

Did you ever play in the sprinkler or hose?

August 11

Share an experience about
poison ivy, poison weed,
bee stings or bug bites.

August 12

Did you have any favorite family songs that you sang together?

August 13

Tell of an experience climbing a mountain or a big hill.

August 14

Share a memory of staying overnight with a friend.

August 15

If you ever ran away from home, tell about it.

Do you remember being really curious about something?

August 17

Share your childhood experiences with roller skates.

August 18

Did you ever experience home sickness?

Tell about a favorite, or least favorite baby-sitter you had.

August 20

*Share an early experience
with shaving.*

August 21

*Tell about a favorite doll,
teddy bear or other stuffed toy.*

August 22

What other kinds of toys did you play with?

August 23

Did you have to abide by a curfew as a youth?

August 24

Describe any "follow the leader" games you played.

August 25

Phones have changed over the years. Describe how you used a phone to call up a childhood friend.

August 26

Did you ever have a fire in your home or accidentally catch something on fire?

August 27

Tell about going to box socials or pot lucks.

August 28

Tell about an incident when you were very angry with your mom or dad.

Tell about an incident when your mom or dad was very angry with you.

August 30

*Share a memory
involving an outhouse.*

August 31

Do you remember any
Labor Day traditions of your youth?

September 1

V J Day...Do you have a memory involving the end of World War II? If not, then share a memory of Vietnam.

September 2

Back-To-School-Days...
What do you remember about that
big yearly "First Day of School"?

September 3

*Tell about your school
year calendar.*

September 4

Tell about a school bully.

September 5

What do you remember doing at recess?

September 6

Tell about the playground equipment at your grade school.

September 7

Did your parents ever make you wear something stupid to school?

September 8

Tell about who you thought was the smartest kid in school and why.

September 9

Tell about the naughtiest kid in school.

September 10

How did you experience
the 9/11 attacks?

September 11

September 12

*Name the schools
that you went to.*

What was your most embarrassing school moment?

September 14

Name the Grade School
teachers you remember.

September 15

Name the Jr. High teachers you remember.

September 16

*Name the High School
teachers you remember.*

September 17

Describe a typical school day outfit in grade school...

In high school...

September 18

Where did you usually buy the clothes you wore?

If you were ever in a fight, tell about it.

September 20

If you ever had a hero,
tell who and why.

September 21

*Tell about a teacher who
meant a lot to you and why.*

September 22

Were there any negative role models who influenced you?

September 23

How did you get to and from school?

September 24

What were your school colors?

September 25

What was your school mascot?

September 26

Tell any sports you played in Jr. High or High School.

What was your favorite sport to participate in or watch?

September 28

What was the biggest physical problem you had to deal with?

September 29

Do you remember a school custodian?

September 30

What is the worst trick that you remember a student playing on a teacher?

What is the meanest thing you ever saw a teacher do to a student?

October 2

Tell about your school lunches.
Did you have a lunch box?
What did you eat?

October 3

*Did you ever have a crush
on a teacher?*

October 4

Do you have any special memories about raking and burning leaves or mowing the lawn?

October 5

If you ever played in the leaves, tell about it.

October 6

Do you have some good
advice for me?

October 7

October 8

Share some good advice that <u>you</u> have received in your lifetime.

October 9

October 10

Relate a story about a mouse in the house.

October 11

Share a memory about a bat in the house.

October 12

What allowance did you get at different ages during your youth?

Did you have to do anything to earn it?

October 14

*Do you have any advice on
how to be wise with my money?*

Tell about pulling or losing a baby tooth.

October 16

Did you ever lose something really important to you?

October 17

Did you ever lose or break something that belonged to someone else?

October 18

Did you ever have a "good friend" who did something mean to you?

October 19

Share a favorite fall memory.

October 20

Did you ever pick apples?

October 21

What is the farthest you ever ran or walked?

October 22

Did your High School
have cheerleaders?
What did they wear?

October 23

Can you recite any of the school cheers?

October 24

*How did your school
observe Homecoming?*

October 25

Do you have any special
Homecoming experiences to relate?

October 26

Tell about any other High School extra-curricular activities.

October 27

Tell a story about a time when you dressed up in a costume.

October 28

Share a memory about being very scared.

What did people do at Halloween?

October 30

Do you have a special Halloween memory?

October 31

Did you ever tell ghost stories?

November 1

Do you have a good ghost or haunted house story to relate?

November 2

*Tell about how you first
met my grandmother.*

November 3

What qualities first attracted you to her?

November 4

Tell about your wedding day.

November 5

*What would you like me
to know about my Mom?*

November 6

*What would you like me
to know about my Dad?*

November 7

Tell me about the
day I was born.

November 8

Who was the President
when you were born?

November 9

When did you cast your first Presidential vote and for whom?

November 10

Veteran's Day...
Name the veterans in your family and times during which they served.

November 11

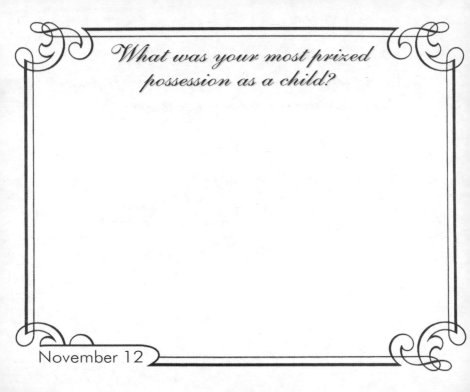

What was your most prized possession as a child?

November 12

Do you have a story about standing up against odds for something you really believed in?

Did you ever feel a hatred for another person? Explain.

Tell about the best birthday present you ever received.

November 15

Was an injustice
ever done to you?

Did you ever make a purchase you later regretted?

November 17

Tell about a memorable birthday cake.

Have you ever had a recurring dream?

November 19

Did you ever chew tobacco?

November 20

*Did you have
a watch as a child?
What was it like?*

November 21

Many people remember just what they were doing when they heard of the assassination of John F. Kennedy. If you are not old enough to have that time etched in your memory, relate any other childhood story.

November 22

Share a memory about a weather-related school cancellation.

November 23

Tell about Thanksgiving
traditions of your youth.

November 24

What foods were on your
Thanksgiving table?

November 25

*Share a favorite
Thanksgiving memory.*

November 26

Do you have any ice skating memories to share?

*What hobbies or collections
did you have as a youth?*

*Tell about the day
my parent was born.*

November 29

How did you choose the name for that child?

Please list your children's full names and dates of birth.

December 1

*On the next pages,
please share some stories
about raising my parent.*

December 2

December 3

December 4

December 5

December 6

Pearl Harbor Day...
If you are not old enough to relate
a memory of that day, relate
any other childhood remembrance.

December 7

Tell about your favorite store to browse in as a youth? What did you like to look at there?

What did you first buy using your own money?

December 9

Tell about something you built, designed or made as a youth.

Were you ever in a church or school Christmas or Holiday pageant?

December 11

(If the following Christmas topics
do not apply, please share your special
Holiday memories and traditions.)

Where did you get your
Christmas trees and
when did you put them up?

December 12

Tell about how you decorated your Christmas tree.

December 13

Did you hang a Christmas stocking?

December 14

Did your grandma or grandpa ever make gifts for you? What?

December 15

*Did your mom or dad
ever make gifts for you? What?*

December 16

Tell about the best
Christmas present you ever received.

December 17

*Tell about something
special you gave to your mom.*

Tell about something special you gave to your dad.

*Tell about the worst
Christmas present you ever received.*

December 20

Tell about your experiences
with Santa Claus.

December 21

Did you ever go Christmas caroling?

December 22

Did your family observe the birth of Jesus at Christmas? In what ways?

Tell about Holiday celebrations at a relative's house.

December 24

Do you remember a
"best" Christmas?

December 25

*Share any other
Christmas memory.*

December 26

*Do you remember celebrating
any special wedding anniversaries
of your parents or grandparents?*

December 27

Is there anything else that you would like me to know about your childhood?

December 28

December 29

What special memories do you have of New Year's Eve or New Year's Day?

December 30

If you were to make a
New Year's Resolution this year,
what would it be?

December 31

Memory Journals for Special People

Grandma, Tell Me Your Memories

Grandpa, Tell Me Your Memories

Mom, Share Your Life With Me

Dad, Share Your Life With Me

To the Best of My Recollection

To My Dear Friend

My Days...My Pictures

My Days...My Writings

My Life...My Thoughts

Heirloom Edition – Grandma, Tell Me Your Memories

Heirloom Edition – Mom, Share Your Life With Me

Heirloom Edition – To the Best of My Recollection

Sisters

Mom, Tell Me One More Story...Your Story of Raising Me

Dad, Tell Me One More Story...Your Story of Raising Me